The Romantic Era

The Life, Times, & Music Series

The Romantic Era

The Life, Times, & Music Series

Peter O. E. Bekker, Jr.

Friedman/Fairfax Publishers

A FRIEDMAN/FAIRFAX BOOK

ISBN 0-9627134-5-7

THE LIFE, TIMES, & MUSIC SERIES: THE ROMANTIC ERA
was prepared and produced by
Friedman/Fairfax Publishers
15 West 26th Street
New York, New York 10010

Editor: Nathaniel Marunas
Art Director: Jeff Batzli
Photography Editor: Grace How
Production Director: Karen Matsu Greenberg

Designed by Zemsky Design

Printed in the United States of America

Contents

Introduction

Opinions differ about the boundaries and ingredients of the Romantic era, because Romanticism evolved at different times in the different arts and because it was a period of intense personal expression that nevertheless expanded upon artistic styles of the past. Beginning in the 1750s and continuing until about 1850, visual artists produced in a style that is now called "Romantic." Romantic literature began appearing around 1800 and remained a potent force for the next thirty-five years.

Musically, Romanticism's seeds were planted during the Classical era (1750–1820) by composers such as Carl Philipp Emanuel Bach (1714–1798), a son of the Baroque era (1600–1750) master, Johann Sebastian Bach (1685–1750), whose own music was favorably reassessed by many of the Romantics.

A *piano ad incorporating illustrations of famous composers of the Romantic era.*

C.P.E. Bach's work inspired the two most prolific composers of the Classical period: Wolfgang Amadeus Mozart (1756–1791) and Franz Joseph Haydn (1732–1809). Mozart in particular anticipated the Romantic form, if there is such a thing, with several of his minor-key compositions, especially the Symphony No. 40 in G Minor, K. 550 (1788), and the Piano Concertos in C Minor, K. 491 (1786), and D minor, K. 466 (1785), which to the casual listener might sound much more like Beethoven than Mozart. There is no question that Haydn and Mozart were both substantial influences on the young Ludwig van Beethoven (1770–1827), who more than anyone else is credited with guiding and transforming music from high Classical to the passionate and much more personally ardent form that came to be called Romantic.

Beethoven's practice piano.

Ludwig van Beethoven (1770–1827)

One of the outstanding composers of Western music, Beethoven was a transitional figure linking the formal, structured Classical era with the emotional, free-form Romantic era.

Beethoven's work falls roughly into three periods. The first encompasses compositions up to about 1800 and includes his first two symphonies, three of his five piano concertos, twelve of his thirty-two piano sonatas, the Violin Sonata in A Minor ("Kreutzer"), Op. 47 (1803), and six of his sixteen string quartets. In structure, these mostly follow musical conventions established in the Classical era; stylistically, they owe quite a lot to Haydn (with whom Beethoven studied in Vienna) and to Mozart (whom he admired).

It was in his second period, roughly 1800 to 1815, that Beethoven transcended the Classical model and established himself as a unique and formidable voice, particularly with the completion in 1804 of his Symphony No. 3 in E-flat (the "Eroïca"), Op. 55 (1803).

Originally called "Bonaparte," the Symphony No. 3 was probably inspired by Beethoven's view of Napoleon as a great liberator because of the latter's French Revolutionary and military campaigns against monarchs and tyrants. However, the symphony was first performed without a title; legend has it that Beethoven was so disillusioned by news of Napoleon's coronation that he changed the dedication to read "[an] heroic symphony to celebrate a great man."

Much longer than any previous symphony, this piece broke conventions with its vast scale, its compulsive rhythms, and the fervor of its finale.

Even though Symphony No 4 in B-flat, Op. 60 (1806), reverted to Classical structure, the remainder of Beethoven's symphonies—all but the final, No. 9, were completed by 1815—were again guided by passion and emotion. The explosive Symphony No. 5 in C Minor, Op. 67 (1808), contrasts sharply with the serene Symphony No. 6 in F (the "Pastoral"), Op. 68 (1808), yet both are ruled by the main

Manuscript of Beethoven's beloved "Moonlight" sonata.

The village of Mödling, near Vienna, where the completely deaf Beethoven composed the Symphony No.9 and Missa Solemnis.

precepts of Romanticism. The Fifth is a turbulent, nearly unbridled declaration that man can conquer fate; the "Pastoral," a "programmatic" potpourri of orchestral representations of Nature, portrays a violent thunderstorm, a babbling brook, and the ceaseless humming and buzzing of tiny things.

Beethoven himself represented the Romantic ideal of a heroic figure who battled valiantly against tragic circumstances. Aware by 1800 that he was losing his hearing, Beethoven described his feelings of despair, resignation, and ultimately defiance in letters to friends and his two brothers. To his brothers he wrote that he was determined to "seize fate by the throat."

Though his career as a concert pianist was ended by total deafness, Beethoven nevertheless continued to compose from 1815 until his death in 1827. Those twelve years saw the completion of five piano sonatas, the last five string quartets, the *Missa Solemnis*, and the stunning Symphony No. 9 in D Minor (the "Choral"), Op. 125 (1824), which features a triumphant choral finale. Grossly misunderstood at the time of its debut, the Ninth is now considered one of the great wonders of Western music.

It was during this later period, especially in the string quartets, that Beethoven took the greatest liberties with Classical structure, foreshadowing the more emotionally expressive innovations that the Romantics would make. Beethoven experimented with diverse harmonies and incorporated as many as seven movements—as opposed to the traditional four—into his quartets. In addition to varying the number of movements, Beethoven also varied the "moods" that Classical composers had assigned to each; for example, he would often substitute a "cynical" theme for the traditionally playful *scherzo* movement.

Beethoven remains a paradox. In his fierce independence, dramatic musical experiments, and struggle to overcome personal adversity, he was perhaps the original artist-hero so revered by the Romantics. He was an inspiration for later composers such as Richard Wagner, who found it important to teach and sometimes preach through art. At the same time, Beethoven never completely rejected his early adherence to Classical principles of composition. Beethoven is most appropriately remembered not simply as a gifted proponent of any particular school, but as a towering musical figure whose creations and influence transcend characterization and continue to inspire.

Revolutionary Times

Because Romanticism was more an overall artistic movement than a particular, definable style of music, art, or literature, its parameters are very difficult to nail down. It evolved at a revolutionary time in Europe: the British and French were still feeling the economic and political effects of their involvement in the American Revolution (1775–1783) and both nations were destined for even more drama in the one hundred years that followed; the French Revolution (1789–1799) toppled the monarchy in favor of a more representative government, but at a cost of years of violent unrest that included the Reign of Terror (1793–1794) at home and the French Revolutionary (1792–1802) and Napoleonic (1803–1815) wars abroad; the Industrial Revolution was beginning to transform the continent from rural, agrarian states into a collection of powerful, modern nations; and nationalism, not surprisingly, was on the rise.

Converging at the turn of the nineteenth century, these incendiary social and political developments were only preludes to the coming conflicts brought about by the fundamental upheavals in both technology and culture. For instance, Italy's Risorgimento (1796–1870)

Above: Liberty Leads the People (1830), *an example of Delacroix's flamboyant style.*

The Revolutions of 1848

Economic recession, crop failures, and political frustration in the middle class led to a rapid series of revolutions throughout Europe in 1848.

The first flare-up occurred in France on February 24th, when Louis Philippe, the last French king, gave up his throne and went into exile in England. A minor demonstration the day before had mushroomed into an insurrection, and Louis Philippe found himself without either political or military support. He had ruled nominally as a constitutional monarch, but had winked at the parliamentary system and established a strong personal rule during his eighteen years on the throne by manipulating elections, granting special favors, and selecting malleable premiers. His reluctance to sanction a more responsive and representative government was deeply at odds with the economic and political requirements of an industrializing France, a shortsightedness that caught up with him in February of 1848. The Second French Republic was declared immediately upon Louis Philippe's abdication.

Louis Philippe

News of this from Paris prompted a similar revolt in Austria, where popular demonstrations forced Klemens von Metternich, Austrian Minister of Foreign Affairs, from office. This inspired nationalistic revolts in territories usurped by the Austrian Empire; Hungary gained autonomy on March 5th, prompting the Croats to sue for independence from Hungary. In Italy, where the Risorgimento had long been lobbying to oust foreign occupiers from its northern provinces, a Venetian Republic was declared, followed quickly by a revolution in Milan that was supported by the liberal regime in Sardinia. In June, nationalistic Czechs formed the Pan-Slav Congress to press for equality with the Germans, but none of this lasted for long. The Czechs were put down by Austrian forces almost immediately; a month later, Austria regained control of Milan. By the middle of the following year a new Austrian emperor, Francis Joseph, had established a harsh centralized government and had convinced the Russians to thwart the Hungarian independence movement. The Roman republic declared by Giuseppe Garibaldi and Giuseppe Mazzini collapsed, and the Austrians quickly retook Venice.

Europe was swept by revolutions in 1848.

The U.S. Civil War (1861-1865)

The U.S. Civil War is remembered now as a war of unification. Its effects were felt most acutely in the United States, but the ugly and bloody conflict attracted considerable international interest not only because of the new nation's growing stature, but because the outcome would determine the terms of the world's access to the raw agricultural materials in the South, particularly cotton.

The United States hovered on the brink of the Industrial Revolution as the Civil War began, and emerged four years later as a world power. In a global context, the timing and many of the provocations that led to the conflict mirrored what was happening elsewhere as nations jockeyed for advantage in an industrializing world. The South entered the battle to preserve its agrarian, almost feudal way of life—a way of life that would prove hopelessly outmoded by the end of the conflict.

Both sides showed skill and resourcefulness not only in battle, but also in diplomacy, which surprised the many Europeans who followed the war avidly. Southern diplomats had great success lobbying European donors for money and munitions. Northern diplomats showed equal sophistication by deftly blunting the diplomatic successes of their opposite numbers. France, Britain, and several other European powers constantly debated entering the war on one side or the other. It is a testament to the worldliness of Northern and Southern diplomats that through cajolings, promises, and threats, they were able to keep the Europeans mostly on the sidelines. The North won a particularly critical concession when Britain agreed that blockade-running ships bought by the South, and under construction in Scotland, be kept in their Scottish ports until after the war.

Among many other things, the U.S. Civil War marked the end of innocence for the United States. In the years that followed, the United States joined the family of nations for whom industrialization, expansion, and international intrigue became the keys to prosperity.

Above: Currier and Ives capture the fury of the U.S. Civil War in The Battle of Sharpsburg.

was a nationalistic unification movement sparked by Napoleon Bonaparte's invasion and occupation of northern Italy. The Revolutions of 1848 were prompted by economic recession and festering, nationalistic yearnings throughout Europe. The Crimean War (1853–1856) was a British and French reaction to Russia's plans for expansion into the Balkans.

Recessions and the rising tide of nationalism led to insurrection and revolt throughout Europe in 1848.

Prussian nationalism gave rise to Otto von Bismarck's German Empire in the Seven Weeks' War of 1866, and the Franco-Prussian War (1870–1871) toppled the Second French Empire.

The continent was recast during the nineteenth century and the turmoil was felt and reflected by the Romantic artists, who came to define as their fundamental idea the sanctity and relevance of the individual.

General George Washington takes command of the Revolutionary Army.

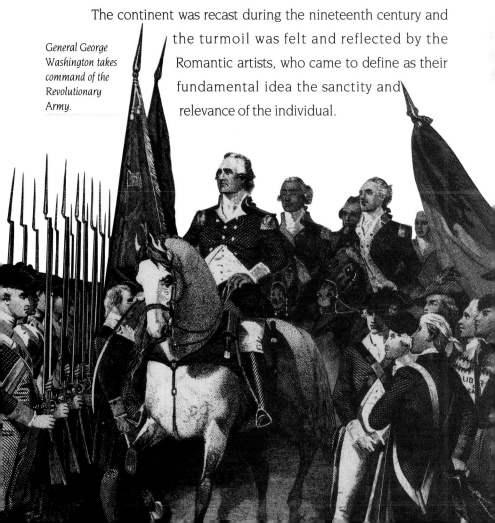

The Crimean War (1853-1856)

Another in a long series of battles between Russia and Turkey, the Crimean War was unique because of the involvement of Britain and France, both of which ultimately allied with the Turks against the Tsar. The underlying concern in this conflict, as in all of the Russo-Turkish wars, was the nettlesome "Eastern Question": how to divide the territories of the crumbling Ottoman Empire without upsetting the European balance of power. But the Crimean War had an abundance of subscripts that further complicated an already complex situation.

Russia was interested in expanding into the Balkans, which were at that time still part of the Ottoman Empire. Britain was worried that such a move would jeopardize its lucrative Mediterranean and Asian trade route through the Bosporus Strait. The French were concerned about access to certain Christian shrines in Constantinople (Istanbul) and other Ottoman cities. The religious issue also interested Russia, which was trying to reassert its protectorship over millions of Eastern Orthodox subjects in the Ottoman Empire.

Long negotiations ultimately failed. Russia made the first military move by occupying two Turkish principalities. Ignoring an ultimatum from Turkey to withdraw, the Russians instead destroyed the Turkish fleet at what came to be called the Sinope Massacre. Inflamed by this aggression, which was quickly reported by the new communications medium, telegraphy, citizens of Britain and France clamored for war. Their governments complied.

The next big question was where to hold the war. It was eventually decided to send an expeditionary force of Turkish, French, and British troops to the Russian Black Sea fortress at Sevastopol on the Crimean Peninsula. Fighting commenced but it was a sloppy war without distinction on either side. Most of the casualties were from disease, not battlefield wounds. The futility and the many military blunders were recorded in Alfred, Lord Tennyson's "Charge of the Light Brigade."

Sevastopol fell in September 1855. The Russians agreed to stiff reparations in the Treaty of Paris the following year. The Black Sea was demilitarized to guarantee Britain's trade routes there. Russia abandoned its claim as protector of Balkan Christians, satisfying the French. The Ottoman Empire, for the moment, remained intact, though shaken.

COSSACKS OF THE DON.

The Original "Me" Generation

If anything sums up the Romantic ideal, it is the notion of an inner muse. Painters, writers, and musicians began cultivating and listening to their "inner voice" for inspiration. Musically, it was a time of exuberant, imaginative composers such as Franz Liszt, Frédéric Chopin, Robert Schumann, Johannes Brahms, Giuseppe Verdi, and Richard Wagner, many of whom favored expressive musical content over strict musical form. Virtuoso solo performers such as pianists Liszt and Clara Schumann (1819–1896), wife of Robert, and the violin master Niccolò Paganini (1782–1840) were looked upon as heroes and heroines. Eugène Delacroix (1798–1863) and Francisco de Goya (1746–1828) were among the visual artists who explored imaginary, exotic, ethereal, and supernatural themes. The English writers Lord Byron (1788–1824) and Percy Shelley (1792–1822) were acutely idealistic and exalted the Romantic "cult of individualism" in both their lifestyles and work.

Above, top: Delacroix often featured exotic, non-European characters in his paintings, as in Donne di Algeri nelle loro stanze *(1834). Above, right:* Fair Rosamund and Queen Eleanor *(1866) by Sir Edward Burne-Jones (1833-1898), who described his works as "romantic dreams."*

The New Muse

The veneration of individual expression represented a major change in the way art had traditionally been inspired and produced. Artists of earlier periods usually relied on wealthy patrons or institutions such as the Church for commissions

Dante Gabriel Rossetti (1828-1882), a founder of the pre-Raphaelite school, painted Monna Vanna *in 1866.*

and support. This meant they were often forced to honor many spoken and unspoken rules of "acceptability" that had little to do with artistic merit. The rules ranged from adherence to the ideals of Church doctrine to considerations as mundane as recognizing and honoring a patron's whims, tastes, or even vanity. Artists violated the rules at their own peril; some were jailed, banished, or killed for biting the hands that fed them. While there is no question that creative artists of earlier eras produced inspired, monumental, magnificent work, it was mostly in the service of others; the Romantics, in contrast, served themselves.

The Seven Weeks' War (1866)

The European Revolutions of 1848 did not accomplish much for the instigating groups except in one important area: their rhetoric and blood served as an enduring inspiration for subsequent reformers. The Seven Weeks' War (also called the Austro-Prussian War) was an opportunity for Italian nationalists to resume the fight against Austrian occupation. Primarily a war by Prussia against Austria, Italy allied itself with Otto von Bismarck and together they engineered a series of quick victories against Austrian and some German troops.

The battles began in June and by the end of August, the Treaty of Prague awarded several German states to Prussia. The treaty also replaced the German Confederation of 1815, a group dominated by Austria, with the North German Confederation dominated, not surprisingly, by Prussia.

While the main outcome of the Seven Weeks' War was the elevation of Prussia to preeminence among the German states, Austria was also forced to cede Venice to Italy under the terms of the Peace of Vienna.

Franco-Prussian War (1870-1871)

Prussia continued its push for dominance in Europe in a campaign that brought down the Second French Republic and set the stage for the rise of the *Deutsches Reich* (German Empire).

Although ostensibly at odds over the Hohenzollern candidate for the Spanish throne, France went to war against Prussia in July of 1870 mostly because Otto von Bismarck's policy of aggression in Europe threatened French security.

The conflict was engineered by Bismarck, who hoped to throw a scare into the southern German states that had not yet joined his North German Confederation by drawing France into a war. The ultimate goal was to complete the German unification he had begun in 1866 in the Seven Weeks' War against Austria. He was entirely successful.

By editing a diplomatic telegram to Napoleon III, Bismarck suggested that a routine meeting with a French diplomat had degenerated into an exchange of insults. France was left with the options of suffering diplomatic humiliation or going to war.

Otto von Bismarck

Completely unprepared to face Bismarck's war machine, the French suffered immediate and substantial setbacks. After little more than a month of fighting, Napoleon III surrendered himself and his Army of Sedan to Bismarck, thus effectively ending the Second French Republic.

Despite the quick formation of a Third Republic and a Government of National Defense in Paris, the capitol came under siege and the war ended on Prussian terms. Bismarck demanded the election of a national assembly that reflected French opinion on the course of the war. In the balloting that followed, a large majority voted for peace. In the Treaty of Frankfurt, France was compelled to pay a staggering indemnity of five billion francs and also to cede to Prussia all of the province of Alsace and part of Lorraine.

Bismarck's victory was total. The southern German states joined his confederation and on January 18, 1871, in the Hall of Mirrors at Versailles, a new German Empire was declared that would dominate Europe until its defeat in World War I.

A *newspaper illustration of the siege and bombardment of Strasbourg.*

The Industrial Revolution

Although not itself a war, the Industrial Revolution definitely contributed to several conflicts that occurred during the nineteenth century. As they became aware of the profits possible through the production and sale of factory-manufactured goods, governments became aggressive in protecting their markets or in staking claims to new sources of raw materials. As in any other era, this aggression was often cloaked by diplomatic smoke-screens, and wars of greed were more often than not called something else.

The Industrial Revolution started in Britain, mostly through a series of coincidences, and quickly spread throughout Europe. An increasingly prosperous middle class was demanding goods that the traditional handcrafting trades were unable to make. Casting about for new ways to capitalize on the demand, entrepreneurs developed the factory system using disparate technological developments such as John Kay's flying shuttle, invented in 1733; James Hargreaves' spinning jenny, invented in 1764; and Edmund Cartwright's machine loom, invented in 1785.

Once the juggernaut got rolling, it was impossible to stop. Each innovation led to an immediate demand for others and in the late

1700s there began a cascading series of related and unrelated inventions, discoveries, and fundamental changes in the structure and goals of Western society. James Watt's refinement of the steam engine made large-scale manufacturing possible from about 1780. This led to an increased demand for coal and iron, which in turn led to a demand for a more reliable metal, met by Sir Henry Bessemer's process for making steel. Roads were improved, canals were built, and railroads were developed to facilitate the transportation of raw materials and finished goods. Economies and livelihoods were transformed as banking, insurance, and investment took on new significance as the essential oils of the new prosperity. The world literally changed during the nineteenth century, practically overnight. The transformation brought with it a multitude of problems, many of which are still with us: pollution, exploitation, and economic instabilities and inequities. Even with the advantages of experience and hindsight those substantial dilemmas remain daunting. During the nineteenth century, when they first occurred on a wide scale, these dilemmas were terrifying to a world innocent of the ravages of an industrialized society.

Above: The Bessemer steel converter.
Left: Watt's steam engine.

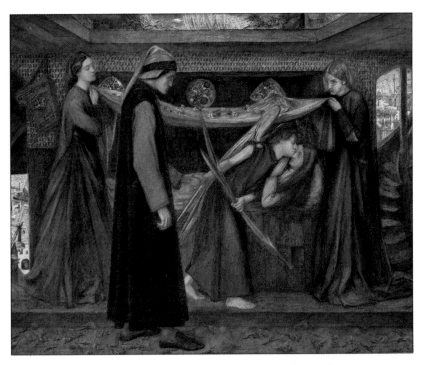

The dramatic increase in prosperity throughout Europe, brought about by worldwide colonization and the Industrial Revolution, provided a comfort zone for the kind of introspection and self-expression that propelled the Romantics. The Church had lost considerable control over peoples' lives: there was an eager middle class clamoring to attend concerts and to buy books and paintings. Artists were freed from perpetuating in their work the dogma of the institutions that once supported them; they were also freed from the restrictions that those institutions had often placed on their creative expression. They came to value these new freedoms as central to the creative process and did not hesitate to exercise them.

Above: Dante's Dream at the Time of the Death of Beatrice (1856), *Dante Gabriel Rossetti. Left: The heavy influence of his friend Dante Gabriel Rossetti can be seen in Sir Edward Burne-Jones'* The Baleful Head (1886-1887).

Romantic Music

Music of the Romantic era is distinguished by its dramatic, expressive, exaggerated, often grand eloquence. Building on the traditional forms for opera, the symphony, and, to a lesser extent, oratorios and concerti, the Romantic composers moved away from the strict technical and intellectual exercises of the Baroque and Classical eras and transformed music into a free-form vehicle for the broad expression of human emotion. Baroque and Classical listeners marveled at the technical skill and cleverness of their era's composers; the Romantics were more interested in plumbing the deep, primal well of emotional involvement through the expressive power of music.

Above: Interior of Milan's legendary La Scala Theater, circa 1859.

Vocal Music

Thousands of art songs were written by the Romantics. These were short, expressive pieces, usually for piano and single-voice accompaniment, that often set the lyrics of such poets as Byron, Goethe, Heinrich Heine (1797–1856), Paul Verlaine (1844–1896), Stéphane Mallarmé, and Charles Baudelaire (1821–1867) to music.

The pre-Romantic composer Franz Schubert (1797–1828), pioneered the *lieder* form of art song, which ultimately evolved into the song cycle, a longer form in which music was written for a group of poems, usually by the same author or on the same topic.

Robert Schumann was a prolific Romantic era composer of *lieder* and song cycles, producing in a single year (1840) *Dichterliebe* ("Poet's Love"), Op. 48, and *Liederkreis* ("Song Cycle"), Op. 24, based on the poems of Heine; another *Liederkreis*, Op. 39, based on the tales of Josef von Eichendorf; and *Frauleinliebe und Leben* ("Woman's Love and Life"), Op. 32, from a story by Adelbert von Chamisso (1781–1838).

Short, stylistic solo pieces without vocals were invented or adapted for the parlor and concert stage chiefly by Chopin, Liszt, and Schumann. These included dances and études, which were written mainly for piano but also for violin. Dance forms included waltzes, mazurkas, polonaises, and polkas. Études were originally training exercises for students of the piano that in the nimble hands of Liszt and Chopin evolved into a virtuoso concert medium.

Opera in the Nineteenth Century

During the Romantic era, for the first time since the form's development, opera became music for the masses. It was art that could entertain, overwhelm, and even provoke political revolt, as the Dutch discovered in 1830 when the Brussels premiere of *La muette de Portici* ("The Deaf Girl of Portici"), by Daniel Auber (1782–1871), helped to ignite the Belgian independence movement.

The great themes of the Romantic era found their most persuasive voice in opera, whose main centers were in Italy, France, and Germany. Opera was, after all, the most elaborate art form, encompassing instrumental music, singing, acting, storytelling, poetry, painting, and stagecraft. The German composer Richard Wagner thought of opera in just that way and called his creations *Gesammtkunstwerk,* "total artwork." Opera attracted the finest musical practitioners and fired the public's imagination.

Grand Opera

Grand opera was an innovation that developed in France mostly through the efforts of Gasparo Spontini (1774–1851), a transplanted Italian, and another foreigner, the German composer Giacomo Meyerbeer (1791–1864). Based on tragic or dramatic themes and staged as a flamboyant spectacle, grand opera was the perfect response to the demand in France by a flamboyant, spectacle-loving middle-class for epic stories, lavish productions, dazzling scenery and special effects, a thunderous chorus, and plenty of choreography.

Spontini's *Fernand Cortez* (1809), an opera suggested by Napoleon Bonaparte, even featured marching armies and live horses onstage. Aside from eye-popping spectacle, the absence of any spoken dialogue was a feature that distinguished grand opera from the other styles popular in nineteenth-century France: *opéra comique* and *opéra bouffe.* Every line in a grand opera is sung. Auber's *La Muette* is an example. Meyerbeer's *Les Huguenots* (1836), *L'Africaine* ("The African Woman," 1865), and *Le Prophète* (1849) are all grand operas, as is Gioachino Rossini's *William Tell* (1829).

Gasparo Spontini

French Comic Opera

Despite its name, opéra comique was a form that usually dealt with serious or sentimental themes, and if it was funny, its humor was dark or cynical at best.

Not as visually overwhelming as grand opera, opéra comique featured spoken as well as sung dialogue. The wrenching tragedy *Carmen* (1875), by the French composer Georges Bizet (1838–1875), was an exceptionally popular opéra comique in its day, and remains so even now.

Opéra bouffe on the other hand, like its older Italian cousin, *opera buffa,* was usually based on light, funny, sentimental, or even satirical themes. There is not much distinction between opéra bouffe, which was already an established form

Georges Bizet

at the dawn of the Romantic era, and *operetta*, which developed during the last half of the nineteenth century. Both feature dancing, singing, and spoken dialogue. The French composer Jacques Offenbach (1819–1880) wrote more than one hundred operettas, among them *Orphée aux enfers* ("Orpheus in the Underworld," 1858), *La belle Hélène* ("Beautiful Helen," 1864), and the less flippant (and unfinished) *Contes d'Hoffmann* ("Tales of Hoffmann," 1881).

Operettas remained a popular entertainment into the twentieth century, attracting composers like Richard Strauss (1864–1949) and the British team of William Schwenk Gilbert (1836–1911) and Sir Arthur Sullivan (1842–1900), whose musical satires such as *H.M.S. Pinafore* (1878) and *The Pirates of Penzance* (1880) continue to delight audiences in every English-speaking country. Operetta was imported to the United States in the early twentieth century by transplanted Austrians and Germans who had gone there to live and work. As musical theater it became a forerunner of the contemporary Broadway musical.

Above: Scene from Carmen: *"Escamillo arrives with Carmen." Below: Madame Bressler-Gianoli in the role of Carmen.*

Instrumental Music

The piano was the instrument of choice for most Romantic composers. Its extensive dynamic range and ability to express passages loudly, softly, or at any dynamic in between made it an ideal instrument for solo and orchestral work. The Romantic era was flooded with piano compositions, unleashed by Beethoven's monumental piano sonatas and variations of the early 1800s. While the piano was heard nearly everywhere in nineteenth-century music, the Romantic composers generally favored single-movement piano pieces over the multi-movement sonatas of Beethoven, Schubert, and their Classical predecessors.

Steinway grand fortepiano.

One prime contribution of the Romantics was the character piece, a kind of program music in which instruments "act out" the parts of characters or "describe" the action. The musical fairy tale *Peter and the Wolf*, Op. 67 (1936), by the Russian post-Romantic composer Sergey Prokofiev (1891–1953), is a familiar example of narrated program music in which a storyteller introduces different instruments that play specific themes that represent the characters.

Character pieces generally did not include narration. They were written both as solo compositions for piano or violin and as orchestral works for full-size or scaled-down ensembles. In addition to the flow of the music itself, composers generally used two other elements to express mood, action, and emotion: a descriptive title for the

Italian Opera

It was to opera that Italian composers made most of their contributions during the nineteenth century, forsaking other forms of music for the one that was born in Florence around 1600 and flourished in the ensuing two hundred years, developing into a national and international institution.

Roles for great singers remained dominant. The Romantic era was the golden age of *bel canto* ("beautiful singing") in Italian opera, in which elaborate and emotional arias generally stole the show.

Because of its firm national character and strong traditions, Italian opera was less influenced by Romantic era conceits than music elsewhere. While elements of French grand opera made inroads, for example, in the growing importance of the orchestra and chorus, Italian composers generally stuck to the tried-and-true *opera seria* and *opera buffa* forms, at least in the first half of the nineteenth century. The eminent Italian composers wrote in both forms. Toward the end of the century, *verismo opera* ("reality

opera") would catch fire, along with the nationalistic opera seria of Giuseppe Verdi (1813–1901).

Opera seria was "serious" opera that usually dealt with mythological or heroic themes. Established during the Baroque era by Alessandro Scarlatti (1660–1725) and taken up by composers as diverse as George Frideric Handel (1685–1759) and Wolfgang Amadeus Mozart, the popularity of opera seria spread quickly throughout Europe. Distinguished by the formality of its presentation, plots were advanced through arias that alternated methodically with recitatives (a kind of singing that resembles speech). Orchestras in opera seria were used almost exclusively as support for the vocalists rather than as the formidable tool they had become in grand opera.

Gaetano Donizetti (1797–1848) wrote the *seria* operas *Lucrezia Borgia* (1833) and *Lucia di Lammermoor* (1835), among others. Vincenzo Bellini (1801–1835) wrote eleven operas, all of which were serious and highly emo-

A scene from Act II of Verdi's Rigoletto. *Covent Garden, London, 1911.*

Scene from Puccini's Madama Butterfly.

tional; *I Puritani* ("The Puritans," 1835) and *Norma* (1831) are his two most well-known works. Chopin was said to have admired Bellini's lyric style.

Opera buffa was a light-hearted form that evolved from the *intermezzi* of more serious operas. It was customary for short, comic sketches to be performed between the acts of opera seria. The plots of these intermezzi were usually unrelated to the main opera and even to each other, very much as the antics of clowns who wander around a circus ring between acts are unrelated to the performances of the circus stars. Sometimes though, the intermezzi *would* be related, telling a comic story in two or three parts between the acts of the overriding tragic story. The little comic "operas within an opera" eventually evolved into opera buffa.

Gioachino Rossini (1792–1868) wrote some of the most memorable opera buffa: *Il Barbiere di Siviglia* ("The Barber of Seville," 1816), *La Gazza ladra* ("The Thieving Magpie," 1817), and *La Cenerentola* ("Cinderella," 1817), for example. Donizetti contributed *Don Pasquale* (1843) and *L'Elisir d'amore* ("The Elixir of Love," 1832). Giuseppe Verdi's *Falstaff* (1843), his final work, was his only opera buffa.

Verdi, whose long career gave him plenty of opportunity to experiment with different approaches to the form, is remembered as the most daring and original Italian opera composer. In early works such as *Rigoletto* (1851), *Il Trovatore* ("The Troubadour," 1853), and *La Traviata* ("The Erring One," 1853), Verdi wrote in traditional opera seria style. But with *Aïda* (1871), written to celebrate the opening of the Suez Canal, he began to provide dramatic roles for the orchestra and he minimized the often stark distinctions between arias and recitatives to help bolster character development. The pinnacle of this experimentation was *Otello* (1887), based on Shakespeare's play.

Verismo opera developed at the very end of the Romantic era and stretched into this century. It presented a realistic picture of life and featured everyday people embroiled in violent or melodramatic situations that could conceivably happen to anyone. Among the composers of verismo opera are Ruggiero Leoncavallo (1858–1919), whose *I Pagliacci* ("The Clowns," 1892), remains one of opera's greatest tear-jerkers, and Giacomo Puccini (1858–1924), whose *La Bohème* (1896), *Tosca* (1900), and *Madama Butterfly* (1904) remain popular today.

work, as in Debussy's *La Mer* ("The Sea," 1905), and program notes written by the composer to outline what the music was supposed to convey. Among the many kinds of character pieces are rhapsodies, impromptus, preludes, nocturnes, and laments.

Another major contribution of the Romantics was the symphonic poem, invented by Franz Liszt. Based on the program symphony (a character piece for full orchestra written in the traditional multimovement symphonic style), symphonic poems, also called tone poems, generally have just one long movement. Liszt's first such composition was titled *Ce qu'on entend sur la montagne* ("What One Hears on a Mountaintop," 1857) and was inspired by a Victor Hugo poem. Claude Debussy's *Prélude à l'après-midi d'un faune* ("Prelude to the Afternoon of a Faun," 1894), inspired by the poem by Stéphane Mallarmé (1842–1898), is another example of a symphonic poem. The French composer Hector Berlioz (1803–1869) is credited with introducing the first program symphony in 1834—the energetic and startling *Symphonie fantastique*, Op. 14 (1830).

Above: Yvonne and C. Lerolle at the Piano, *by Pierre Renoir.*

Robert Schumann (1810–1856)

Schumann's interest in literature was nearly as great as his interest in music. He pursued both from an early age, writing piano compositions, poetry, prose, and drama while still a schoolboy. He was well-served by those exercises later in life, displaying a formidable sensitivity to the relationships between music and words, particularly in his *lieder* and song cycles, but also as a commentator and critic of the contemporary music scene.

Schumann was a founder of the influential *Neue Zeitschrift für Musik* ("The New Music Journal"), based in Leipzig, in which he repeatedly criticized the program music and music drama of Liszt, and later of Wagner. Schumann no doubt was responding to Liszt's overwhelming influence during the Romantic era, which caused much hostility among those who either were not anointed as disciples of the "new German music" or simply objected to what they saw as Liszt's gratuitously unorthodox, flamboyant approach. Schumann, like Chopin and Brahms, was not a musical "anarchist," and preferred a more conventional approach to composition.

From all accounts Schumann was high-strung, the result of a busy life, and also perhaps of emotional problems. He described his own nature as divided between gentle and impulsive. He worried constantly about his mental health and spent time in an asylum shortly before he died.

Schumann wanted desperately to become a concert pianist, but gave up all hope of that when he permanently injured his hand in a device intended to stretch and strengthen his hands. Turning to composition, he eventually completed four symphonies, the opera *Genoveva,* Op. 81 (1818), a concerto for piano and violin, some chamber music, an overture and incidental music, Op. 115 (1848), for Goethe's play *Manfred,* and incidental music, Op. 148 (1853), for another Goethe play, *Faust.*

Schumann's wife Clara, daughter of his piano teacher Friedrich Wieck (who opposed their marriage), was a popular and successful concert pianist who kept up a hectic touring schedule except during the years of her marriage, when she bore seven children. She returned to the concert trail after Schumann's death; her repertoire centered mostly on Schumann, Brahms, Bach, Mozart, Beethoven, and Chopin.

Schumann is most remembered today as a *lieder* composer and for his elegant, playful piano compositions such as *Fantasiestücke* ("Fantasy Pieces"), Op. 88 (1842), *Blumenstücke* ("Flower Pieces"), Op. 19 (1839), *Kinderscenen* ("Childhood Scenes"), Op. 15 (1838), and *Humoreske* in B-flat Major, Op. 20 (1838). The *Fantasiestücke,* Op. 73, was written in the remarkably short period of three days (February 11-13) in 1849; Schumann originally conceived this for the clarinet but the published score indicates that either cello or violin would be a suitable alternative.

German Opera

The nineteenth century saw two kinds of opera in Germany; the German Romantic form in the first half and another kind of Romantic spectacle in the second: Richard Wagner's flamboyant music drama. German Romantic composers borrowed heavily from their Italian and French colleagues but made far greater use of the Romantic fascinations with medieval myths and legends, fairy and folk tales, and occult, mystical, and supernatural themes.

The central figure in the transition from *Singspiel* (traditional German comic opera of the eighteenth century) to German Romantic opera was Carl Maria von Weber

Richard Wagner.

(1786–1826), who broke ground in 1821 with *Der Freischütz* ("The Freeshooter"), an opera that combined supernatural horror with folksongs, colorful orchestration, and tranquil scenes of country life.

Weber pioneered a fuller use of the orchestra to enhance the story lines of his operas and also to help develop characters. His sense of melody was such that several of his tunes became German folk songs. Weber was an early proponent of *leitmotif*, which is a particular musical passage that recurs from time to time and represents a person, place, idea, or object. It was a device used extensively by Wagner later in the century.

A list of enduring works in the German Romantic form not written by Richard Wagner would include Beethoven's *Fidelio*, Op. 72 (1805), Ludwig Spohr's *Faust*, Op. 60 (1816), E.T.A. Hoffmann's *Undine* (1816), and Robert Schumann's *Genoveva*.

Richard Wagner (1813–1883)

In the second half of the nineteenth century, German opera was completely dominated by the operas of Richard Wagner and by his underlying philosophy that opera should be a unification of all the arts. He called his opera

music drama and dedicated the greater portion of his creative life to unifying music, literature, the visual arts, and stagecraft in productions he called *Gesammtkunstwerk*, a German word meaning "total artwork." Wagner's vision was that music and story should have equal importance and that each must always work to enhance and advance the other. Evidently not content to let his work speak for itself, Wagner even wrote several treatises on his artistic philosophy, the most poignant of which are *Das*

Kunstwerk der Zukunft ("The Artwork of the Future," 1850) and *Oper und Drama* (1851).

Like the other Romantics, Wagner used his orchestrations to express feelings and to convey themes, but his approach was radical. Gifted with a flair for lovely melody, his sense of harmony was not the predictable kind favored by his predecessors, in which lilting melodies were pleasingly resolved by returning to the original key of the passage (tonal). Wagner's harmonies often contained notes from unrelated musical keys (chromatic), and they sometimes seemed to lose all reference to any particular key (atonal).

He significantly expanded the size of the orchestra and invented instruments to accomplish his aims when conventional appliances didn't measure up. The Wagner tuba is one such, invented for the four-opera series *Der Ring des Nibelungen* ("The Ring of the Nibelungen"), comprised of *Das Rheingold* (1854), *Die Walküre* (1856), *Siegfried* (1871), and *Die Götterdämmerung* ("The Twilight of the Gods," 1874).

View from the box seats at the Metropolitan Opera House, New York, in the 1890s.

Instead of dividing his operas into songs and scenes as other composers had always done, Wagner got rid of the set-piece aria and instead employed "endless melody," in which there was one continuous line of story and music throughout the production. He wrote the texts (librettos) of all his operas, delving into medieval history and Teutonic myth and legend for plots and characters.

Not surprisingly, Wagner was criticized by many of his contemporaries who were stunned by what he was doing to opera. The main complaints were that his operas were overly sentimental and entirely too long. But Franz Liszt was an active champion of Wagner (who married Cosima, Liszt's daughter). Mostly through Liszt's efforts, the Bayreuth Festival Theater was built and opened in Wagner's lifetime (1876) expressly to accommodate the hefty production demands of Wagner's work. The Bayreuth Festival continues to feature the Wagnerian operas that in addition to the Ring cycle include *Rienzi* (1842), *Der fliegende Holländer* ("The Flying Dutchman," 1843), *Tannhäuser* (1845), *Lohengrin* (1850), *Tristan und Isolde* (1859), *Parsifal* (1882), and *Die Meistersinger von Nürnberg* (1868).

Siegfried awakens Brunhild, a scene from Der Ring des Nibelungen.

Franz Liszt (1811–1886)

An unprecedented piano virtuoso and one of music's first "superstar" performers, Franz Liszt attracted paying throngs to public recitals where, after the show, he was often mobbed by admiring fans.

These days Liszt is remembered as the inventor of the symphonic (tone) poem—his *Prometheus* (1850) and *Hamlet* (1858) are examples—and as a pioneer of the program symphony.

Born in Raiding, Hungary, Liszt showed great musical promise as a child, and started giving piano concerts by the age of nine. A year later his family moved to Vienna where the young Liszt studied with Beethoven's disciple Carl Czerny, and also with another prominent musician of the time, Antonio Salieri. But Liszt was denied admission to the Paris Conservatory (because of his youth and perhaps also because of his foreign birth), a development that put an end to his formal piano instruction.

Nevertheless, Liszt spent half his lifetime giving piano recitals, astounding audiences throughout Europe with his volcanic, incredibly dextrous performances. Many of the piano studies (études) he wrote were so technically demanding that contemporaries urged him to simplify them so they could be played by others.

Despite his renown, Liszt was a courtly and generous man, though sometimes snobbish and definitely contradictory. Late in life he took four minor orders on the way to becoming a Catholic priest and often lamented to friends that he should have attended seminary. He also never married and his domestic arrangements scandalized many. He lived for a time with Countess Marie d'Agoult, and later with Princess (by marriage) Carolyne von Sayn-Wittgenstein, both of whom had left their husbands to be with him. His daughter Cosima, one of three children by Marie d'Agoult, would later cause a similar scandal by leaving her husband, the conductor Hans von Bülow, to live with the composer Richard Wagner.

Liszt was a generous philanthropist, contributing and raising money for various charities, not all of them related to music. He helped Robert Schumann and Frédéric Chopin by playing their large piano works when each was unable to do so; Schumann because of damage he had done to the fingers of his right hand in a finger-stretching device and Chopin because he suffered from tuberculosis and was frequently ill. Liszt published a biography of Chopin after his friend's death, though some suspect the actual writing may have been done by Princess Carolyne.

An active supporter of the musicians he admired, Liszt conducted all of Beethoven's symphonies and championed the controversial 9th symphony, which at the time of its debut was considered by many to be the misguided mumblings of a deaf man. Liszt was also an active supporter of Richard Wagner, another controversial composer, and produced the

Liszt conducts a new oratorio. Pest, Hungary.

latter's *Tannhäuser* and the world premiere of *Lohengrin*. He successfully lobbied on Wagner's behalf for construction of the Bayreuth Festival Theater to properly present Wagner's monumental operas. (Ironically, Liszt died while attending the Bayreuth Festival in the summer of 1886.) Hector Berlioz and Camille Saint-Saëns (1835–1921) also benefited from Liszt's efforts to promote the public performance of their unconventional music.

Liszt had contact with nearly every major musical figure of his day, either personally or by letter. He allied himself with important musical causes, writing articles and books to put forth his ideas. In great demand as a teacher, students came to him from all over Europe and the United States.

The nineteen *Hungarian Rhapsodies* (1851–1886) are probably the most familiar of Liszt's compositions. Vividly a celebration of his Hungarian roots, the rhapsodies are most likely based on tunes that were popular in Hungarian cities at the time they were written. Other Liszt compositions include the symphonic poems *Tasso* (1849), *Les Préludes* (1854), and *Mazeppa* (1854); *Eine Faust-Symphonie* (1857); a symphony to Dante's *Divina Commedia* (1867); oratorios and masses; and nocturnes, piano concertos, and études.

Liszt's music room.

Orchestral Music

The symphony orchestra grew to its largest size ever during the Romantic era. Instruments were added to each of the four sections—strings, brass, woodwinds, and percussion—to bolster their resources for texture, color, harmony, melody, and intensity.

To the woodwinds were added contra-bassoon, piccolo, bass clarinet, and English horn as well as extra oboes, flutes, clarinets, and bassoons. An array of colorful instruments, including cymbals, chimes, bells, gongs, triangles, and castanets joined the timpani in the percussion section. No new kinds of instruments were introduced into the string section, but the number of players was increased to balance the more powerful brass and woodwind choirs. Expressive playing techniques such as *pizzicato* (string plucking),

double-stopping (playing two notes at the same time), and *tremolo* (rapid repetition of a single note) were used extensively. The advent of valves for brass instruments improved their versatility. Trombones, trumpets, tubas, and four traditional horns rounded out the typical orchestra.

Like other kinds of music, the symphony lost its formal Classical structure during the Romantic period and became a fertile field for the personal expression of the composer. The tradition of having four movements was often overlooked; some symphonies had three, others five, and the symphonic poem had but one. Greater

Opposite, above: Tuba. Opposite, below: Oboe.
Above: The orchestra grew in both size and importance in the Romantic era.

Frédéric Chopin (1810–1849)

A prodigy and later a concert pianist whose fame equaled that of Franz Liszt, Chopin is remembered today for his piano literature—more than two hundred compositions in such forms as sonatas, concertos, preludes, nocturnes, études, ballades, and dances (especially waltzes, polonaises, and mazurkas).

Born in Poland, Chopin lived most of his life in Paris, where he was introduced by Liszt to the French writer George Sand (1804–1876). The pair maintained a stormy ten-year relationship that ended only two years before Chopin's death.

Chopin made frequent use of Polish folk melodies in his piano works, though he never adapted actual folk tunes. His unusual sense of harmony and his ethereal, songlike melodies have made a lasting contribution to piano composition. Liszt in particular was influenced by Chopin's harmonic innovations and his delicate ornamentation. Countless other composers are in his debt, not the least of whom, ironically, are the Impressionists and their nemesis, Richard Wagner.

Manuscript of a Chopin impromptu.

freedom was employed in the internal structure of the movements and a number of composers including Beethoven, Liszt, and Berlioz even took the radical step of writing solo vocal and choral parts into their symphonies.

Symphonic suites—multimovement works that do not adhere to even the broadly interpreted symphonic structure of the Romantic era—were also popular vehicles. All are program works, that is, pieces in which the instruments represent and express identifiable characters, moods, or emotions. Pyotr Tchaikovsky's *Nutcracker Suite*, Op. 71 (1892), is an example, as are A *Midsummer Night's Dream*, Op. 21 (1826) and Op. 61 (1842), by Felix Mendelssohn (1809–1847) and *Sheherazade*, Op. 36 (1888), by Nikolay Rimsky-Korsakov (1844–1908).

Franz Liszt at the fortepiano.

Claude Debussy (1862–1918)

A late Romantic, Debussy founded and was the chief contributor to musical Impressionism, a transitional style that did not attract many followers but nevertheless opened new doors for twentieth-century composers by exploring unconventional harmonies, dissonance, and the five-tone Oriental scale. Mostly, Impressionism was Debussy's personal revolt against what he considered the extravagances of Romanticism.

Debussy attended the Paris Conservatory and won several prizes for his early compositions, including the Prix de Rome for the cantata *L'Enfant prodigue* ("The Prodigal Son," 1884). Even though his life after the age of twenty-five was dedicated to composing, Debussy did not associate with musicians. He preferred the company of painters and writers, faithfully attending the Tuesday evening gatherings at the Paris home of poet Stéphane Mallarmé that attracted prominent Impressionist artists and authors. Mallarmé's poem, *L'après-midi d'un faune* ("Afternoon of a Faun") inspired Debussy's famous prelude of the same name. That piece was the composer's first attempt to tame and refine the Romantic approach to music that in its late stages could be called bombastic.

Mallarmé's work, and the work of the Impressionists in general, was notoriously sparse. Symbolism, and particularly understatement, were important elements in

Debussy's compositions. Still, his work retained many important Romantic elements; many of his compositions are character pieces with descriptive titles such as *Les sons et parfums tournent dans l'air du soir* ("Sounds and Scents Revolve in the Evening Air," 1910), *Feuilles mortes* ("Dead Leaves," 1910-1913), and *Ce qu'a vu le vent d'Ouest* ("What the West Wind Saw," 1910). They are programmatic, colorful, and emotionally expressive.

Debussy wrote twenty-three other preludes. His successful opera, *Pelléas et Mélisande* (1902), in its emotional restraint, is now seen as one of the first substantial broadsides against the dominance of dense, Wagnerian music drama. Debussy's orchestral pieces include *La Mer* ("The Sea"), and *Images* (1912). He also wrote songs, chamber music, a ballet, two books of études, and the *Suite Bergamasque* (1905), which contains what is probably his most familiar piece, *Claire de lune* ("Moonlight").

Maurice Ravel (1875–1937)

A contemporary and admirer of his countryman Debussy, Ravel is also often pigeon-holed as an Impressionist. But his work was far more disciplined than Debussy's and his approach more Classical in the French tradition of polish and clarity. If anything, Ravel was a "neoclassicist," sticking with forms from the Classical era— sonatas, chamber music, and ballet—and applying to them devices popular with the Classical, Romantic, and Impressionistic composers as well as devices of his own. Ravel's late violin concertos, for example, contain bits of jazz.

Like Debussy, Ravel looked to literature for inspiration, admiring the poems of Mallarmé and other contemporary French writers. He embraced poetic and pictorial themes. He employed lively dance motifs, with a special fondness for Spanish rhythms, and he also tinkered with harmonies and dissonance.

By no means a virtuoso, Ravel is nevertheless remembered for his complex piano com-positions; *Pavane pour une Infante défunte* ("Pavane for a Dead Princess," 1899), which he later orch-estrated, is one of his first important works for the instru-ment. One can hear the enigma of Liszt in *Gaspard de la Nuit* ("Gaspard of the Night," 1908), and shades of Chopin and Schumann in *Valses nobles et sentimentales* (1912). The ballets *Boléro* (1928) and *Daphnis et Chloé* (1912) remain popular, as does Ravel's *Rapsodie espagnole* (1908).

The concerto retained its Classical era three-movement structure during the nineteenth century but became much more a showpiece for blistering solo-work. Most concertos were written for piano and orchestra or violin and orchestra.

Concerto overtures, traditionally, were single-movement pieces played as a warm-up before an opera. The Romantic com-posers dropped the opera and used overtures as stand-alone compositions. These too were program pieces, and most had descriptive titles. Tchaikovsky's 1812 *Overture*, Op. 49 (1880), for example, is a musical representation of how Russian troops broke Napoleon's siege of their motherland. The 1812 is a real exercise for the percussion section, where clanging and crashing cymbals symbolizing the sounds of battle drown out the receding strains of the "Marseillaise."

Johannes Brahms (1833–1897)

Because he stuck with strict Classical era construction in most of his compositions, Brahms was called the "Classical Romantic" or the "Romantic Classicist" even in his lifetime. He was called other, less kind things by those in the Liszt-Wagner camp who felt his allegiance to the styles of Mozart and Beethoven was old-fashioned and counterproductive.

Franz Liszt, a leading and fearsome figure of Romanticism, praised Brahms' Scherzo in E-flat when he first heard it in 1853, but the two ultimately came to disagree fundamentally on musical theory. Brahms even signed a manifesto criticizing Liszt and his so-called "Music of the Future."

Brahms had a happier acquaintance with Robert Schumann and his gifted wife, Clara, a concert pianist, that developed into a lifelong friendship. Schumann championed the young Brahms as a great genius of German music and was instrumental in getting his early songs and piano sonatas published.

Born in Hamburg, Germany, Brahms was a gifted pianist at a young age, earning money while still a teenager by playing in taverns and beer halls. His father was a double-bass player with the Hamburg Opera who encouraged his son musically; ironically, opera is the only form Brahms did not attempt. Otherwise, his output, particularly for piano, was vast. He wrote waltzes, variations, and hundreds of *lieder*. His orchestral work includes four symphonies, two piano concertos, two string concertos, chamber works, and concert overtures. He was also a brilliant choral composer; his *Ein deutsches Requiem* ("A German Requiem"), Op. 45 (1868), *Schicksalslied* ("Song of Destiny"), Op. 54 (1871), and *Rhapsodie* for alto, men's chorus, and orchestra, Op. 53 (1869), are still admired.

The most important composer of the Romantic era with an anti-Romantic outlook, Brahms helped revive interest in absolute music, the opposite of program music. That is, he wrote music for music's sake rather than as a representation of emotions, characters, places, or ideas.

"Papa" Brahms at the piano.

Felix Mendelssohn (1809-1847).

Other Major Forms

The Romantics did not contribute much to chamber music or to religious and secular choral music. Chamber music lacked an adequate role for the piano and did not have the format for the colorful and expressive orchestral pieces favored by the Romantics. Still, Antonin Dvořák (1841–1904) and Johannes Brahms, who retained a Classical bent and is called "the Classical Romantic," wrote a respectable number of chamber music pieces.

Brahms, Mendelssohn, Berlioz, Liszt, and Schumann all tried their hand at oratorios. Mendelssohn, a master of choral technique, is considered to have had the greatest success with the form; his oratorios St. Paul, Op. 36 (1836), and Elijah, Op. 70 (1846), are regularly performed today. Nonetheless, the Romantic era is not remembered for its contributions to church music or to choral music in general.

Mendelssohn's manuscript for the finale of Concerto No. 2, Op. 40.

End of the Musical Era

The music of the Romantic era, essentially an ongoing experiment, was eventually assimilated into other styles as composers either responded to nationalistic fevers or honed and refined the innovations of their period into diverse and different schools. Just as there continue to be arguments about Beethoven's place at the beginning of the era, there are also arguments about the late Romantics, some of whom have been classified as niche composers because of their eclectic styles. The Impressionists, Expressionists, and Neoclassicists are examples of these eclectic few.

While "programmatic" and Romantic in most respects, the music of the Impressionists paralleled similar movements in French painting and literature. As Claude Monet and Pierre Renoir were defining impressionistic art in the late 1800s with their outdoor scenes that luminously captured the subtlety of a moment, Claude Debussy and Maurice Ravel were refining the excitable, bombastic Romantic style into a more serene and distinguished form.

Opposite page: The Opera Box, *by Pierre Auguste Renoir. Above:* The "Waltz King,"
Johann Strauss (left), with Johannes Brahms on the balcony of the Strauss home.

Musicology

It was in the relative prosperity of the nineteenth century that music entered the curriculum of many schools for the first time. America led the way in this with Boston setting the pace. Classes in music were introduced there in 1837 and by the middle of the century, most American schools offered courses of one kind or another in music. Training for professional musicians was "formalized" in the United States in the 1860s with the opening of the Peabody Conservatory and the Oberlin College Conservatory.

The academic science of musicology developed partly because of the fascination of the Romantics with the past. Individuals in Europe and America began researching musicians and musical history, mostly as a hobby, sometimes publishing their work in books of limited interest. Raphael Georg Kiesewetter (1773–1850) and Hugo Riemann (1849–1919) were among musicology's pioneers. Harvard's appointment of John Knowles Paine as Professor of Music in 1875 marks the "formalization" of musical study at the academic level.

John Knowles Paine.

Nationalism was a movement involving Romantic composers who hoped to create a distinct style—based on folk idioms—that glorified nationalistic ideals. The movement was born in Russia but was quickly adapted by a handful of composers in Bohemia (Czechoslovakia), Hungary, Rumania, Norway, and Finland. Opera was the primary vehicle for nationalistic music since it provided the best opportunity to tell a succinct story. Mikhail Glinka (1804–1857), the so-called "father" of Russian music, wrote A *Life for the* Tsar (1836), which celebrates the true story of how the first Romanov Tsar's life was saved by a peasant. *Boris Godunov* (1874), written by Modest Mussorgsky (1839–1881) and based on the Pushkin tragedy, is considered the movement's operatic masterpiece.

Mussorgsky was a member of "The Five," a group of Russian composers who actively worked together to promote Russian nationalism through music. Based in St. Petersburg and at work in the 1870s, The Five also included Aleksandr Borodin (1833–1887), Nikolay Rimsky-Korsakov, César Cui (1835–1918), and Mily Balakirev (1837–1910). Tchaikovsky was sometimes called the sixth member of

Pyotr Ilyitch Tchaikovsky (1840–1893)

Renowned in Russia as that country's premier Romantic composer, Tchaikovsky is remembered for his orchestral compositions, among them six symphonies, nine operas, three piano concertos, one violin concerto, and plenty of marches, overtures, and ballets, including the perennial favorites *The Nutcracker, Sleeping Beauty*, Op. 66 (1899), and *Swan Lake*, Op. 20 (1876).

During the Romantic era, most of Tchaikovsky's Russian colleagues were busy writing or touting nationalistic music, a form Tchaikovsky never completely embraced, though he dipped into it from time to time and there is an undeniably Russian "feel" to much of his work. While Tchaikovsky made occasional use of genuine Russian melodies, the overall tenor of his output can be credited more to a fascination with minor-key exposition than with any nationalistic fervor. His marriage to Antonia Miliukova in 1877 led to an emotional crisis that brought him close to suicide. He left Moscow (and his wife) almost immediately after his marriage; friends say he was in an agitated state, but nevertheless he wrote three of his most memorable pieces that year: the Symphony No. 4 in F Minor, Op. 36 (1876), the opera *Eugene Onegin*, Op. 24 (1879), and his violin concerto.

Tchaikovsky taught at the St. Petersburg and Moscow conservatories, both of them newly opened at the time he was hired. He lived both in Russia and the West, traveling internationally as his fame increased, even to the United States where in 1891 he appeared at the opening of Carnegie Hall.

The Nutcracker Prince and Clara; a scene from The Nutcracker.

The Five, though while he sometimes wrote in a nationalistic style, his own outlook, and the bulk of his work, was much more international.

Other nationalist composers of the Romantic era were Edvard Grieg (1843–1907) of Norway, who wrote for piano, orchestra, and chorus; Jean Sibelius (1865–1957) of Finland, who wrote symphonies and symphonic poems; Bedřich Smetana (1824–1884) of Czechoslovakia, who wrote opera, chamber, and orchestral music; and Smetana's countryman Antonin Dvořák, a noted composer of symphonies and chamber music.

The nationalist movement had run its course by the time most cultural historians agree the Romantic era died: 1900. Unlike Romanticism, which continued to influence subsequent styles and musical movements, few composers jumped aboard the nationalist bandwagon. The concept that drove the Romantics—freedom of the individual and the emancipation of individual expression—proved to be a far more enduring philosophy than the single-minded pursuit of national glory.

Impression: Sunrise (1872), *which launched the Impressionist movement, by Claude Monet.*

Romantic Literature

Writers, poets, and thinkers were the true architects of Romanticism. Romantic literature was at its peak during the first thirty years of the nineteenth century, influencing musicians and visual artists with imaginative, fanciful stories that glorified Nature and harkened back to medieval times. Maybe in reaction to the realism of the previous century, which demanded a precise and faithful representation of what the senses beheld, Romantic writers seemed suddenly to lose their rational minds as they veered off precipitously in uncharted directions with only their imaginations as guides. In their work, the Romantics rejected conventional ways of looking at the world. Even in their personal lives some of the famous Romantic writers (Lord Byron for example) were scandalously flamboyant.

Above: Page from Songs of Innocence, *designed and written by William Blake, the visionary poet, painter, and herald of English Romanticism.*

The term Romanticism was adopted from the medieval *romances*, the literature of legends, in which heroic, larger-than-life characters battled adversity in all its forms to win the day for truth, chivalry, and salvation. German poets and writers were more keen to delve into mythology than their English and French contemporaries, who concentrated more on Nature and its importance to Man.

William Wordsworth (1770–1850) and Samuel Taylor Coleridge (1772–1834) are given credit for launching English Romanticism with their short collection, *Lyrical Ballads*, co-published in 1798. In it, the two friends covered ground that would later fire the imaginations of scores of their contemporaries: "Tintern Abbey" is Wordsworth's reflective musing on Man's mystical connection to Nature; in the dreamlike masterpiece "The Rime of the Ancient Mariner," Coleridge creates the illusion of reality from images and events that definitely are not real. John Keats (1795–1821) and Percy Bysshe Shelley sought ideal beauty and truth. Lord Byron mocked the established order through satire and a tumultuous life that ended when he died of fever preparing to help Greek patriots fight against Turkey.

George Gordon, Lord Byron, a gifted and flamboyant English Romantic poet.

In Germany the High Romantics delved deeply into myth, legend, and fantasy. The poems of Johann Wolfgang von Goethe (1749–1832), Heinrich Heine, and Adelbert von Chamisso inspired lieder and song cycles by more than a few Romantic composers, most notably Robert Schumann. Heine's words were an inspiration not only to Schumann, but also to Liszt, Mendelssohn, Brahms, and Wagner, all of whom set them to music in one form or another. The fantastic stories of Ernst Theodor Amadeus Hoffmann (1776–1822) were the basis for Offenbach's *Tales of Hoffmann*, Tchaikovsky's *Nutcracker Suite*, and Schumann's *Kreisleriana*. The operas of Richard Wagner rely nearly exclusively on Teutonic myth and legend.

Romanticism blossomed later in France because of the strong influence of French Classicism and the commotion surrounding the French Revolution and the ensuing Napoleonic Wars. It was also quickly superseded by Symbolism and Aestheticism. Victor Hugo was an early champion of the Romantic style, and his theories are personified in the play *Hernani*, which caused violent partisan quarrels when it opened at

Alcoholism and emotional instability haunted French symbolist poet Paul Verlaine all his life.

Portrait of the poet Charles Baudelaire, by Gustav Corbet.

the Comédie Française Théâtre in 1830. But French Romantic literature is comparatively thin, and many of the writers and poets who
inspired the Romantic composers were Parnassians or Symbolists
such as Charles Baudelaire, Arthur Rimbaud (1854–1841), and
Stéphane Mallarmé.

Johann Wolfgang von Goethe (1749-1832)

Goethe was one of the most versatile thinkers and writers of his or any time. He was born in Frankfurt into comfortable surroundings, but experienced more than his share of crises during his lifetime.

     Goethe became famous in Germany on the strength of the play *Goetz of Berlichingen* (1771), a work of youthful rebellion written when he was just twenty-two. In this work, Goethe criticized, even scorned, contemporary literary and social customs. His fame spread throughout Europe three years later upon publication of *The Sorrows of Young Werther* (1774), a sentimental novel whose core echoed the

Johann Wolfgang von Goethe, one of the greatest writers and thinkers of the age.

sentiment of the French philosopher Jean Jacques Rousseau that society had ruined natural man.

Although remembered most vividly for his dramatic poem *Faust* (Part I, 1808, Part II, 1832), Goethe also produced exquisite lyrical poetry, such as the rich and passionate cycle *Western-Eastern Divan* (1819), which seized the imaginations not only of the public but of other writers, Friedrich Schiller in particular, with whom Goethe ultimately collaborated.

It was during a trip to Italy in 1786 that Goethe decided to

Mountain Passage, *by Caspar David Friedrich.*

dedicate his life to his art. During the decade that preceded his two-year Italian hiatus, Goethe had held a number of high political positions in Weimar in the ducal court of Karl Augustus. Returning there in 1788, he resigned his posts and soon found himself ostracized by court society. It was evidently a painful period, but the isolation had the desired effect, launching Goethe on a course of creative discovery that did not abate until his death at the age of eighty-two.

In addition to *Faust*, Goethe's satire *Reynard the Fox* (1794) was widely admired during his lifetime. Much of his vast output, however, was not appreciated, and is only now getting appropriate recognition; the hexameter *Roman Elegies* (1795) and the lyrical novels *Wilhelm Meister's Apprenticeship* (1795) and *Wilhelm Meister's Travels* (1821) are three examples.

Goethe himself hoped to be remembered as a scientist. He worked not only in pure science but also in social science, anticipating and writing extensively about the effects and societal implications of the Industrial Revolution. Biologists are indebted to his thinking on the structure of animals and plants (morphology), a cornerstone in the theory of evolution. Goethe also wrote a comprehensive history of science that is included in Volume One of his three-volume *Zur Farbenlehre* ("Theory of Colors," 1810) in which he challenged some of the precepts of Newtonian science.

Heinrich Heine (1797-1856)

Heine's *Über Ludwig Borne* ("Concerning Ludwig Borne," 1840). Heine attacked the poet Count von Platen in *Bader von Lucca* ("The Baths of Lucca"), which appears in Heine's third volume of *Reisebilder* ("Travel Pictures," 1826-1831), publicly taunting von Platen about his homosexuality, apparently in response to von Platen's slur about Heine's Jewishness. Heine also took on what he saw as the pretentiousness of Göttingen professors and the pomposity of German aristocrats in *Harzreise* ("Harz Journey," 1826), calling the Hanoverian elite "asses who talk about nothing but horses."

A flamboyant and controversial figure during his lifetime, Heine wrote prose and verse that was both inspiration and basis for scores of compositions by Romantic era musicians. Schumann, Liszt, Mendelssohn, Wagner, and Brahms are among those who generated *lieder,* song cycles, and instrumental and symphonic pieces based on his writing.

Heine's life was not as serene as some of his lovelier poems. There is ample evidence that Heine became increasingly cynical and confrontational, traits that may have been sharpened by the prejudice in German society toward Jews. As he grew older, Heine sharpened his barbs, periodically jabbing at customs, institutions, and even individuals, gaining a reputation as a radical and a hothead.

Heine was expelled from university at Göttingen for dueling. He was later challenged to a duel by Solomon Strauss, who was offended by allegations about his wife in

Like many writers of the Romantic era, Heine venerated Napoleon as a slayer of tyrants. He favored the French occupation of the Rhineland and later expressed admiration for the constitutional monarchy of Louis Philippe, the last king of France. His regard for the new French order led him to take up residence in Paris in 1831, where he continued to write disparagingly about conditions in Germany, as in his epic *Deutschland: Ein Wintermärchen* ("Germany: A Winter Tale," 1844).

Syphilitic and nearly paralyzed for the last eight years of his life, Heine nevertheless produced some of his greatest poetry while bedridden. *Romanzero* ("Romances," 1851) and *Gedichte 1853 und 1854* ("Poems 1853 and 1854") contain some of Heine's most somber and reflective work, as well as his wittiest, most ironic, and most prophetic poetry.

William Wordsworth (1770-1850)

A pioneer in the celebration of the individual, and perhaps the great-est of all English Romantic poets, Wordsworth wrote verse that was a celebration of nature and a chronicle of its influence on human thought and feeling. He is credited with solidifying Romanticism as the major literary movement of his time, even though Wordsworth retreated over the years from his youthful enthusiasm for unbridled imagination. He became uncertain, even uneasy about nature and argued in favor of rationality. But in his youth, and in his so-called "great decade" of 1797-1807, Wordsworth tackled unambiguous social issues and wrote movingly about man and nature as parts of a greater whole.

In "The Ruined Cottage" (1797), Wordsworth addressed the fate of those dispossessed by war and by the Industrial Revolution; the next year *Lyrical Ballads* was published. Three other of his more memorable works were completed in the two-year period 1800-1802: "Michael" (1800), "Ode: Intimations of Immortality from Recollections of Early Childhood" (1800), and "Resolution and Independence" (1802).

Wordsworth spent most of his life in England's Lake District with his sister, Dorothy, whom he relied upon heavily for emotional support. Orphaned by age thirteen, Wordsworth was sent away to school and then to university at Cambridge, though he never earned a degree. He spent 1792 in France, where he halfheartedly joined a revolutionary group. While there he fathered a child by Annette Vallon; he ultimately abandoned them both. He traveled briefly in Germany and spent six years in the south of England, where he met Coleridge. Otherwise, the remainder of his eighty years were spent at Dove Cottage, Grasmere, in the Lake District. Wordsworth was named England's Poet Laureate in 1842.

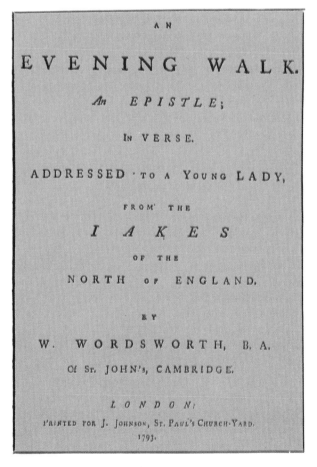

The title page of Wordsworth's "Evening Walk" (1793).

Romantic Art

Visual artists and architects were as much inspired by imagination, self-expression, and a fascination with the past as their creative colleagues in the other arts. The work of Renaissance masters was reassessed early in the nineteenth century and many of their techniques were put to use by the Romantic painters. The grand figures of Michelangelo (1475–1564), the energetic colors of Peter Paul Rubens (1577–1640), and the shimmering landscapes of Claude Lorrain (1600–1682) all found new expression in the nineteenth century.

The symbolic landscapes of German painter Caspar David Friedrich (1774–1840) are Romantic representations of the hills, trees, harbors, and morning mists of northern Germany. They display the subtleties gleaned from a close observation of Nature. Religious mysticism is apparent in *The Cross in the Mountains* (1808), a landscape in which an altarpiece appears incidental to the strong rays of the evening sun.

Above: Francisco de Goya, Self Portrait.

Francisco de Goya's portrait of Maria Teresa de Vallabriga.

Dante and Virgil in Hell, *Eugène Delacroix.*

Eugène Delacroix (1798-1863)

Ferdinand Victor Eugène Delacroix, Self Portrait.

F rance's leading Romantic painter, Delacroix had potent artistic ammunition in the form of the vivid output of his fertile imagination. His work is suffused with spectacular imaginative leaps and unresolved tensions. Exotic characters, mute players in his elaborate and often violent scenarios, populate his more ambitious canvases.

Delacroix often explored the Romantic themes of man's mortality, the uncertainty of life, and the glory of the pursuit of liberty. He sometimes combined these themes, as in *Greece on the Ruins of Missolonghi* (1826), which depicts the defeat of Greek nationalists by the Ottoman Turks (a conflict that led to the death from fever of the English poet Lord Byron, who had hoped to fight alongside the oppressed Greeks). The bloody defeat of what Delacroix considered to be a noble cause appealed to him as the personification of ideal liberty.

The tragedies of Shakespeare and of other, more contemporary writers also appealed to Delacroix. One example is *Hamlet and Horatio in the Graveyard* (1859); it is rife with the symbols and ironies of death.

Delacroix also produced mythological canvases, such as *Dante and Virgil in Hell*, from the series *The Barque of Dante* (1822). He painted conventional, realistic works, mostly portraits, such as the one of his friend, Frédéric Chopin, and his own self-portrait. He was capable of unleashing pure flights of fancy, as in *The Lion* (1861), in which exotic, turbaned men appear with horses and other animals, many of them wild, in a blur of unnatural colors that excite the eye and dazzle the mind.

Scènes de massacres de Scio *is typical of Delacroix's vibrant and often violent imagery.*

Delacroix's contributions were amply recognized during his lifetime. France honored him with the medal of the Legion of Honor in 1831. He was also given lucrative government commissions such as decorating the Chamber of Deputies Library in the Bourbon Palace and the Senate Library in the Luxembourg Palace (both finished in 1847). In 1857, Delacroix was elected to the prestigious Institut de France.

In France, Eugène Delacroix stunned many with exotic, elaborately fantastic, and violent canvases. Baudelaire called him a "volcano artistically concealed beneath a bouquet of flowers." Delacroix's fondness for exotic subjects is especially vivid in *The Death of Sardanapalus* (1828), depicting the death of the last Assyrian king.

It is easier to generalize about the "feel" and content of Romantic music and literature than about Romantic art. The themes and styles are not so identifiable. The Romantic painter Anton Gros (1771–1835) glorified Napoleon's Revolutionary campaigns while Spain's Francisco de Goya bitterly depicted their savagery. The pas-

Goya was not greatly impressed with Madrid's upper classes. Satire seems to be the impulse behind The Family of Charles IV (1800) *in which the regal costumes and vivid background contrast with the fatuous stance of its subjects.*

toral landscapes of Friedrich are considered as "romantic" as the natural disasters—storms, fires, and so on—painted by J. M. W. Turner. Delacroix's sprawling images of rape, death, and plunder hardly seem "romantic" at all.

If the Romantic artists defined themselves in any way, it was in their passion for every mood of Nature and also in their interest in Man's potential for violence. We are left with the message that through our choices we can battle fate to arrive at glory or calamity.

Recommended Listening

Ludwig van Beethoven (1770-1827)
Sonata for Piano in C Minor ("Pathétique"), Op. 13 (1799)
Sonata for Violin and Piano in A Minor ("Kreutzer"), Op. 47 (1803)
Sonata for Piano in F Minor ("Appassionata"), Op. 57 (1807)
String Quartets in F,‹E Minor, C ("Rasumovsky"), Op. 59 (1806)
Fidelio, Op. 72 (1805)
Concerto in B-flat, Op. 19 (1801)
Concerto in E-flat ("Emperor"), Op. 73 (1809)
Symphony No. 3 in E-flat ("Eroïca"), Op. 55 (1804)
Symphony No. 5 in C Minor, Op. 67 (1808)
Symphony No. 6 in F ("Pastoral"), Op. 68 (1808)
Symphony No. 9 in D Minor ("Choral"), Op. 125 (1824)

Vincenzo Bellini (1801-1835)
I Puritani ("The Puritans," 1835)
Norma (1831)

Hector Berlioz (1803-1869)
Symphonie fantastique, Op. 14 (1830)

Georges Bizet (1838-1875)
Carmen (1875)

Johannes Brahms (1833-1897)
Marienlieder, Op. 22 (1857)
Ein deutsches Requiem ("A German Requiem"), Op. 45 (1868)
Rhapsodie, Op. 53 (1869)
Schicksalslied ("Song of Destiny"), Op. 54 (1871)
Academic Festival Overture, Op. 80 (1880)
Symphony No. 4 in E Minor, Op. 98 (1884)

Claude Debussy (1862-1918)
L'Enfant prodigue ("The Prodigal Son," 1884)
Deux Arabesques (1888)
Fantasie (1890)
Nocturnes (1897-1899)
La Mer ("The Sea," 1905)
Prélude à l'aprés-midi d'un faune ("Prelude to the Afternoon of a Faun," 1894)
Pelléas et Mélisande (1902)
Suite bergamasque (1890)
Children's Corner (1907)
Images, Vols. 1 & 2 (1905-1907)
Première rapsodie (1910)
Etudes (1915)

Gaetano Donizetti (1797-1848)
L'Elisir d'amore ("The Elixir of Love," 1832)
Lucrezia Borgia (1833)
Lucia di Lammermoor (1835)
Don Pasquale (1843)

William Schwenk Gilbert (1836-1911), Arthur Sullivan (1842-1900)
H.M.S. *Pinafore* (1878)
The Pirates of Penzance (1880)

Mikhail Glinka (1804-1857)
A Life for the Tsar (1836)

Ruggiero Leoncavallo (1857-1919)
I *Pagliacci* ("The Clowns," 1892)

Franz Liszt (1811-1886)
Grandes Etudes (1839)
Tasso (1849)
Liebesträume (3 nocturnes, 1850)
Prometheus (1850)
Mazurka brillante (1851)
Etudes d'exécution transcendante (1854)
Hungaria (1856)
Les Préludes (1856)
Mazeppa (1856)
Concerto No. 1 for Piano and Orchestra in E-flat (1857)
Concerto No. 2 for Piano and Orchestra in A-flat (1863)
Fugue on the Name BACH (1857)
Hamlet (1858)
Impromptu in F-sharp (1877)
Mephisto Waltz No. 2 (1881)
Twelve Motets (1883)

Felix Mendelssohn (1809-1847)
A Midsummer Night's Dream, Op. 21 (1826), and Op. 61 (1842)
Symphony No. 3 in A Minor ("Scotch"), Op. 56 (1842)
St. Paul, Op. 36 (1836)
Elijah, Op. 70 (1846)

Giacomo Meyerbeer (1791-1864)
Les Huguenots (1836)
Le Prophète (1849)
L'Africaine ("The African Woman," 1865)

Modest Mussorgsky (1839-1881)
Boris Godunov (1874)
Pictures from an Exhibition (1874)

Jacques Offenbach (1819-1880)
Orphée aux enfers ("Orpheus in the Underworld," 1858)
La belle Hélène ("Beautiful Helen," 1864)
Contes d'Hoffmann ("Tales of Hoffmann," 1881)

Giacomo Puccini (1858-1924)
La Bohème (1896)
Tosca (1900)
Madama Butterfly (1904)

Maurice Ravel (1875-1937)
Pavane pour une Infante défunte ("Pavane for a Dead Princess," 1899)
Jeux d'eau (1901)
String Quartet in F (1903)
Miroirs (1905)
Gaspard de la Nuit ("Gaspard of the Night," 1908)
Rapsodie espagnole (1908)
Daphnis et Chloé (1912)
Prélude (1913)
Sonata for Violin and Cello (1922)
Rhapsody for Violin and Piano ("Tzigane," 1924)
Boléro (1928)
Concerto for Piano and Orchestra (1931)

Nikolas Rimsky-Korsakov (1844-1908)
Antar (1875)
Skazka ("Legend," 1880)
Ispanskoe kapriccio (1887)
Voskresnaya ("Easter," 1888)
Sheherazade (1888)

Gioachino Rossini (1792-1868)
William Tell (1829)
Il Barbiere di Siviglia ("The Barber of Seville," 1816)
La Gazza ladra ("The Thieving Magpie," 1817)
La Cenerentola ("Cinderella," 1817)

Robert Schumann (1810-1856)
Papillons, Op. 2 (1831)
Carnaval, Op. 9 (1833-1835)
Toccata in C Major, Op. 7 (1830)
Kinderscenen ("Childhood Scenes"), Op. 15 (1838)
Blumenstücke ("Flower Pieces"), Op. 19 (1839)
Kreisleriana, Op. 16 (1838)
Liederkreis ("Song Cycle"), Op. 24 (1840)
Dichterliebe ("Poet's Love"), Op. 48 (1840)
Sechs lieder (for male voices), Op. 33 (1840)
Fünf lieder (for mixed voices), Op. 55 (1846)
Romanzen (for female voices and piano), Op. 69 (1849)
Nachtlied (chorus and orchestra), Op. 108 (1849)
Piano Quintet, Op. 44 (1842)
Piano Concerto in A Minor, Op. 54 (1841, 1845)
String Quartets in A Minor, F Major, A Major, Op. 41 (1842)
Symphony No. 1 in B-flat Major ("Spring"), Op. 38 (1841)
Symphony No. 4 in D Minor, Op. 120 (1851)
Sonata for Violin and Piano in A Minor, Op. 105 (1851)
Fantasiestücke ("Fantasy Pieces"), Op. 88 (1842)
Das Peradies und die Peri, Op. 50 (1843)

Pytor Ilyitch Tchaikovsky (1840-1893)
Valse-caprice, Op. 4 (1868)
Nocturne and Humoresque, Op. 10 (1871)
String Quartets Nos. 1-3 (D, F, E-flat Minor), Ops. 11, 22, 30, (1871, 1874, 1876)
Swan Lake, Op. 20 (1876)
Concerto for Piano in B-flat Minor, Op. 23 (1875)
Concerto for Violin in D Major, Op. 35 (1878)
Eugene Onegin, Op. 24 (1879)
Symphony No. 2 in C Minor ("Little Russian"), Op. 17 (1873)
Symphony No. 6 in B Minor ("Pathétique"), Op. 74 (1893)
Festival Overture ("1812"), Op. 49 (1880)
Sleeping Beauty, Op. 66 (1899)
Nutcracker Suite, Op. 71 (1892)

Giuseppe Verdi (1813-1901)
Falstaff (1843)
Rigoletto (1851)
Il Trovatore ("The Troubadour," 1853)
La Traviata ("The Erring One," 1853)
Aïda (1871)
Otello (1887)

Richard Wagner (1813-1883)
Rienzi (1842)
Der fliegende Holländer ("The Flying Dutchman," 1843)
Tannhäuser (1845)
Lohengrin (1850)
Das Rheingold (1854)
Die Walküre (1856)
Tristan und Isolde (1859)
Die Meistersinger von Nürnberg (1868)
Siegfried (1871)
Die Götterdämmerung ("The Twilight of the Gods," 1874)
Parsifal (1882)

Carl Maria von Weber (1786-1826)
Der Freischütz ("The Freeshooter," 1821)

Recommended Reading

➡ Abraham, Gerald. A Hundred Years of Music, 4th ed. London: Duckworth, 1974.

➡ Einstein, Alfred. Music in the Romantic Era. New York: W.W. Norton & Co., 1947.

➡ Kirby, F.E., comp. Music in the Romantic Period. New York: Schirmer Books, 1986.

➡ Longyear, Rey. 19th Century Romanticism in Music. Englewood Cliffs, N.J.: Prentice Hall, 1973.

➡ Palisca, Claude V. Norton Anthology of Western Music, Vol. 2. New York: W.W. Norton, 1980.

Photography & Illustration Credits

Cover collage images: ©Rudy Muller/ Envision, ©M.K. Rothman/FPG International, Scala/Art Resource; pp. 13 top, 47 top; Bridgeman Art Library/Art Resource, p. 21 bottom; © FPG, p. 45, 57; Giraudon/Art Resource, pp. 10 bottom, 12, 31, 32, 35 top, 38 top, 39 both, 40-41, 42 top, 52, 53, 60, 62-63; Kavaler/Art Resource, pp. 54-55; National Trust/Art Resource, p. 51, New York Public Library, pp. 9, 10 top, 11, 19 both, 25 both, 28, 29, 36, 46; North Wind Picture Archives, pp. 8 bottom, 13, 15, 16, 20, 24 both, 26-27, 33 top, 34, 35 bottom, 37, 38 bottom, 42 bottom, 43 bottom, 50, 58, 59; Courtesy of the Pacific Northwest Ballet, p. 47 bottom; Scala/Art Resource, pp. 14, 17 top, 22-23, 30, 43 top, 44, 48-49, 56, 61, 64, 65, 66-67; Tate Gallery/Art Resource, pp. 17 bottom, 18, 21 top.

Index